WILD WRECKAGE

Charles Cantrell

Červená Barva Press
Somerville, Massachusetts

Červená Barva Press
P.O. Box 440357
W. Somerville, MA 02144-3222

www.cervenabarvapress.com

Bookstore: www.thelostbookshelf.com

Cover Image: Jacob Riis: "Nomads of the Street," Street children in their sleeping quarters, New York (before 1914)

Cover Design: William J. Kelle

ISBN: 978-1-950063-16-1

Library of Congress Control Number: 2020942674

ACKNOWLEDGMENTS

These poems appeared in the following journals, some in different forms. Thanks to the editors.

ABZ: Night Shift at the Teddy Bear Factory
Artful Dodge: Poet for Hire
Ascent: Against Perfection (previously titled From Fat to Happy)
Borderlands: Driving Past Cherry Hill
Buckle &: Sun in an Empty Room
Clackamas Literary Review: Black Spring
Defined Providence: Fueled by Bottles
Dominion Review: 1510 Talleyrand Avenue (previously titled 1510 Talleyrand Avenue, Jacksonville, Florida)
English Journal: The Mad Bomber Dreaming He's Henry David Thoreau, Words Never Said
Exit 7: Beautiful River, Dirty Water
Flyway: Dark Roast
G.W. Review: Richard Hugo Won't Be Appearing Tonight
Green Hills Literary Lantern: X Equals the Unknown
Illuminations: In a Dark Time…, When the Miraculous Doesn't Happen
The Hurricane Review: Map of the Arctic at the AA Meeting, Canine Epiphany
The Laurel Review: Ball-Peen
The Licking River Review: Shrimp
The Literary Review: Wittgenstein's Hut
The Mid-America Poetry Review: Gulls Above Prison Walls
MARGIE: Fluctuations
Mississippi Valley Review: Soul
Mudfish: Lorca in New York; My Macho Double
New Delta Review: Orpheus Buys a Harley; Running Backwards
New Zoo Review: Anatomy 101
Off the Coast: Mama Speaks from the Grave
Paterson Literary Review: Marilyn Monroe to Arthur Rimbaud
Plainsongs: Snake Pantoum
Poetry Northwest: An Unprayed-for Song
Poem: Green Fuse
Portage Magazine: Desert Snow
Prairie Schooner: Silage; God and the Windshield Washer

Quarterly Review of Literature-Singapore: Should the Moon
Quercus Review: Retirement Matters
Rattle: Sartre in the Hayloft
Rivendell: Elegy for the Factories and Trees of Bristol, Virginia
Rosebud: The Knife-thrower's Lady
The South Carolina Review: Blank Slate; Suzi's Teddy Bear, Dark Art
Southern Poetry Review: Did Kafka Ever Drop a Failed Story
(previously titled Kafka's Janitor)
Square Lake: Ruby
Thorny Locust: Holiday
ucity review: Breakfast and Dog Walk
White Pelican Review: Viable Twigs
Wisconsin Review: Blue Hammer, Bruises

"An Unprayed-for Song" and "Did Kafka Ever Drop a Failed
Story" also appear in *Wisconsin Poetry*, an anthology issue of
Transactions, published by *Wisconsin Academy of Sciences, Arts and
Letters*, 1991.

"Green Fuse" in *Encore*: More of Parallel Press Poets-2005.

"Retirement Matters" also appears in <u>75 Poems on Retirement</u>,
University of Iowa Press – 2007.

"Marilyn Monroe Replies to Arthur Rimbaud" won Honorable
Mention in 2010 Allen Ginsberg Poetry Awards.

Cicatrix – chapbook published in 2001, Parallel Press.

Thanks to the Wisconsin Arts Board, Ragdale, Ucross, The
Vermont Studio Center, and the Virginia Center for the Creative
Arts for grants, scholarships and fellowships which aided in
completion of this manuscript. Thanks over the years to Frank
Boyer, Charles Boyer, Mark Kraushaar, Kenny Zamora Damacion,
Susan Herport Methvin, John Minczeski, Francine Sterle, Carolyn
West, Jeannie Bergmann, Ron Czerwien, Richard Roe, Richard
Merelman, and especially Jeanie and Steve Tomasko.

TABLE OF CONTENTS

I.

II.

III.

IV.

For my wife, Pat, and my two children, Julie and Marc

Wild to be wreckage forever
—James Dickey

WILD WRECKAGE

I.

1510 TALLEYRAND AVENUE

Drunk, my father picked up a skillet
and lunged at my mother. She ducked
into my room and called the police.

Two burly men threw my father, swinging,
down the stairs. A week later
he lifted his bandage and showed me the stitches,

like a tiny railroad atop his scalp.
I stared at that catgut,
wanted to unravel it, make it go away;

make the wound come clean,
white as the window pane weeks back
when my father taught me to draw my name.

"Now watch it disappear," he said,
blowing enough breath to hide *Charles*.
He watched my lip turn down.

"But you can write it again," he said,
like this, his finger poised like a pencil.
He exhaled, then drew the half moon

of my first letter so wide I saw the night:
street lights on palm-lined curbs,
tugboats and dock lights dancing on the river

in the distance. Refocusing, I saw my father
smiling. "Now you write the rest," he said.
He held my hand and I wrote.

SHRIMP

A hump of rope darkens the shrimp boat's bow.
        Shrump-shrump, the engine turns.
               Brine teases my nostrils—dripping nets
piled deck-side. My father waves
        from the rail—thousands of shrimp
               for canneries restaurants, but I don't care,
don't particularly like shrimp
        and often balk at the fishy scent
               woven to Dad's shirt, hands, under
his nails. "It's a job," he said, "and I love it.
        If you don't eat shrimp, you don't like me."
               So I try to see those near translucent
wigglers as creatures, human size,
        from outer space, in movies I love.
               The sauce, blood red and vinegary, helps.
The more I eat the more Pop smiles
        Shrimp, shrump, hump of *hemp*:
               sounds I love. If I rolled those words
across my tongue, I bet I could taste them.
        The jellied flesh, followed by a French fry
               or sip of orangeade, isn't so bad,
and who hasn't lied for love?

BLANK SLATE

Huckleberry, hollyhock, loblolly,
honeysuckle, my mother said from the porch,
not in the same sentence. The way she twanged
those syllables between puffs of an Old Gold
stopped me from mowing, stopped an oriole
from singing in the cherry tree.

If I said her words drifted toward the shade
beneath the cherry's branches, flapped their sweet,
colloquial wings, I wouldn't be lying.
I stepped into the shade, mopped my brow,
heard *Get back to mowing*, but those
other words massaged my inner ear.

I had my sweet time and loved it.
Clouds drifted, blue sky expanded.
Those words—alliterative, liquid—drove
even deeper. And of course there's no honey
dripping from my body, no smoke, of course,
curling toward a blue sky in my body.

RUBY

Our cuckoo clock wouldn't work,
and when my mother turned it over a wing fell off.
Teary-eyed, she asked me to glue back the feathers,
Then she sang, "Tiger, tiger burning bright…"
Said, "The tiger's me. I'd like to put on my red dress
and go dancing at the Green Frog,
but your dad's still jangling keys."
He worked nightwatch at the auto plant.

My mother worked a broom under the sofa,
where, she swore, armies of spiders plotted overthrow.
Of what? I didn't know. My head in a comic,
she walked by, whispered, "That will turn your brain
to oatmeal." She put on a record, said, "I'll teach you
to dance." A violin sounded off key, the needle
etching a deeper groove on Tennessee Waltz.

Where crescendo should've moved me, I pouted,
backing away. She danced back and forth,
cigarette between her lips.
Though she wasn't wearing her red dress,
she danced and smoked and labored for love,
holding her arms out in a circle.

CANINE EPIPHANY

What's the point when I'm not supposed to
point? Two dogs, one behind the other,
stuck together, between cinder blocks
behind an abandoned church. "Don't point,"
said my mother. But I couldn't help it.
"Why's that dog hurting that other dog?"
Tongues lolled, saliva dripped, tails stood
straight up. I wanted to know all about those
dogs. Shouldn't they have been playing
with tennis balls, or just chasing one another—
anything but this? Especially the one in front,
black and wiry, the size of our rat terrier,
bleeding from behind. My mother jerked me ahead.
"They aren't hurting each other," she said—
though the female growled and the male
pumped away and nipped her neck—
no shame, no guilt, naked despite fur.
My blunt question with my stiff finger
drawing nothing but, "I said don't look at them.
Look at the stained glass windows, the red and purple.
That's St. Francis, patron saint of—"
But I wasn't listening. Two yelps, then two
barks going in two directions. I wanted to
look back, but her hand was behind my head
and pushing. Would I get some pizza?
I was hungry as a wolf.

MAMA SPEAKS FROM THE GRAVE

Honey, wear nice shoes,
like I taught you. People
often judge from the ground up.

Grab clouds from the sky.
Remember how you loved
my sweet potato pie?

Grow some sweet potatoes.
See what happens. Open
your arms, more, wide, wider.

Love is big, needs room.
You own more room than you know.
Keep readin' and learnin'

but watch the loneliness part.
A heart in a shut room
ain't that alive, ain't beatin'

loud enough. But a quiet heart's
another thing. It's a peaceful one.
Do you hear it? Don't lie.

FUELED BY BOTTLES

With his hammer
that smashes rusty nails
sparking miniature stars
visible in daylight

With his level
and the sliding yellow eye
that wants to bob true
but the board is warped
or the ground's not right

With his rage
fueled by bottles
I don't understand and stay
clear of his breath
of rotting apples

With his kindness
that comes with a black coat
he hangs on my bedpost—
my first pea coat, and I will dare
the snow to find an opening

With his fear of losing
a job while my mother
wipes his hung-over brow
with a yellow washcloth
as I watch for the school bus

With his spine
rogue cells begin *to* devour
and he can't shake enough salt
and cayenne on his beans

And his regret
like a tough weed
growing beside a knotty fence post
that will take no nail
without bending it.

GREEN FUSE

Bored with long division, I pictured the blue bicycle—
   —used, bent chain guard I could fix—
     but my mother wouldn't buy it,
because Dad, drunk again at work, lost his shipyard
   pipefitting job. My mother got hired at Franklin's
     as a seamstress. I wept, wept at my sick cat, falling
grades, most anything. A distant station on my radio
   broke in with a taped program of someone named Dylan
     Thomas. Scratchy bass, not unlike Dad's whiskey-bruised
and smoke-sanded vocal cords.
   "Young and easy under apple boughs" escaped me,
     but I liked the sound. Looping sentences sped me
on a roller coaster, saying young and wild were ok, even good,
   that green fields blossomed beans and grain, daisies and corn,
     then died but burst again.
I didn't know what I was hearing was poetry.
   My mother returned to check my work. "The Force…"
     winding down, she stood there, hands on hips, head
cocked to one side. I was wondering what that force was that
   drives just about everything.
     She said, "You'll know about lovers soon enough,
especially the trouble they cause. Turn that off."
   The tape was over anyway. She checked my problems.
     For a change, I got more right than wrong.
That last poem I couldn't figure, but something told me life
   is a *whoop* and a *holler* despite math phobia,
     a green brain's tears, a father who said
little more than "Don't come home with dirty clothes, you're
   too skinny to hit a home run, just get on base, I'd take you
     fishing, but you talk too much, ask your mother
to help you…" I wouldn't call it love that "dripped
   and gathered," and *whoops* and
     hollers were a long way off.

DARK ART

I took art and began to color
everything black. My teacher, Mr. Lock,
pipe-cleaner arms and legs, voice like a jay,
shrilled, "Aren't black roses a bit much
even in, what do you call this, hard bitten
realism?" I couldn't answer. Charred clouds hung

like an umbrella over houses. I loved houses,
sometimes I chalked in a dog in the yard,
black lab after a black bone. Jet rain
drenching black trees, black summer leaves.
The blacker my work the lower my grades.

Dad drank, clutched the blanket
on his bed the way he clawed sand on Omaha Beach,
hallucinating Nazis from D.T.'s.
Mom cried, threw his shirts out to keep him
from leaving to buy more wine, but he said
"to hell with it" and left shirtless.

He died that spring on the railroad tracks,
drunk, smashing his skull on a rail.
My paintings got blacker: creeks, cows
in a field, hawk on a stump…all black
except for a gray sky topped with purple cirrus.
Mr. Lock stopped yelling at me, though I

turned in a totally black drawing
despite a silver hangnail moon in the upper left.
"At least there's some light in this," he said
and gave me a C. In May I drew some flowers, red,
yellow, violet, near houses, almost
smiling, with shutter-like teeth.

X EQUALS THE UNKNOWN

"Words or silence are all we have,"
the famous writer says on the talk show,
then lowers her head, as if in prayer, humility?
The host nods, keeps nodding,
lights making her gray coat shine, as if
the chinchilla is alive in the twilled fur.

Talk or no talk, like my father, quiet yesterday,
in the chill chopping wood. I was picking up maple,
smelling the pulp as I hauled the chunks to the porch
and stacked them. Maybe all we have is snow and wood
and the orange juice I'm sipping for my cold—
too sick to go to school, flunking algebra

and no one to help. I turn off the TV
and picture the dead blue jay I found
in pine needles, pulled some feathers
and tacked them in a circle above my bed—
my own kind of silence. Artistic, I thought.
My mother comes in: "I don't give a damn

if you're sick or not. You're going to school
tomorrow and ask that teacher for help."
I picture myself watching out the rear window
squiggles the bus tires print in the snow,
rolling toward unknown numbers experts say
hold the secrets of the universe.

BLUE HAMMER

I found it in the snow.
I'd use it for my shop project:
a puppy box. I kept the hammer
under my bed. My older brother
thought everything I owned—bike,
marbles, ball gloves—was his.

I took planks from an abandoned
lumber yard. Dad had saws, nails and,
of course, hammers, but I went
into the garage with my hammer
and buzz-rip, buzz-rip, pound,
pound, pound…produced a square box.

My dog, Susie, was due any day.
The box wasn't level. Bent nails—
I hammered them in that way.
So what if I got a "C."
After the pups were born,
I put the tool under my pillow.
Watch out, intruders, even in
dreams. My hammer, often on the sheet

beside me, caught in moonlight on chrome,
and the blue handle sometimes
had a fist around it. I could
size a body up fast. Even the molecules
were dangerous in the blunt tip
of my lovely hammer,
saved from a white oblivion.

BALL-PEEN

Because my father lost his job
nailing boxes shut, drunk, he flung
dish after dish against the wall.

The police came. After raising his club
one cop got a hammer in the face.
After they yanked my father toward their car

I retrieved the hammer. Recalling my father's
arms waving, I went out under moonlight,
hammer under my belt, handle down like a gun.

Jerking the hammer out, I yelled, "Ain't
no way you fuckers gonna take me.
Nearing a hill I slowed, then threw

the hammer up a slope.
Days later my father made me tell him
where the hammer was. Patting my back

on the way, he asked if I needed help
with fractions. He stood by the fence
while I climbed the hill and found the tool

at the foot of a blackberry bush—
several stems split, berry stains
mixed with dried blood on the head.

BLACK SPRING

After my father died I walked the railroad
where he fell. I walked one rail at least 100 feet
before I lost my balance. I did not stumble,
drunk, like my father. The parallel glare of iron
lifted the sun into my eyes; they began to water.
I looked away and sprinted down the tracks
toward the rough field where my father and I
used to pick blackberries. In the field,
briars on scrubby bushes always tore my trousers.
I wanted to fill my mouth with berries until I
couldn't talk, could hardly breathe
and let the juice run down like black blood,
my blood, more than I needed. Stuff it so far back
that it becomes sweet, letting, I hoped, only good
memories hang on, like those bristled nuggets
that burst in my mouth. In my haste I forgot
it was spring. Nothing but green berries,
no bigger than thimbles, and they hung tight.
I sat on a rock and imagined those berries turning
red then black, and how my father, in a hurry,
placed two cloths on both sides of each bush,
reached inside and shook the limbs for the loose
berries, then showed me how to lift each cloth
into a funnel for the pail.
On the rock I felt water pool
inside my mouth from those imaginary berries.

ELEGY FOR THE FACTORIES AND TREES OF BRISTOL, VIRGINIA

I want to run my nails down the furrowed bark
    of a poplar, disturb woodworms, maybe a downy
        woodpecker. I want to crawl through humus

under barbed wire by a creek to a blackberry clump
    I found as a boy and eat—the indelible juice
        darkening the far parts of my body.

I want to light a cigar by Diamond Matches, closed
    for those who toiled there, coughing blood
        in the unvented acidic air.

I will exhale smoke near Bristol Steel,
    dead as the iron crusting rusted rails,
        and wonder who smashed the last windows

towering over the rail yard.
    I want to lie down in Steel Creek Park,
        drink iced tea, watch kids play ball

while adults flip meat on grills. I might wonder
    why my mother wouldn't let me climb
        our paw-paw tree for the oblong fruit

or yelled when I ate the berries
    from a sugarberry tree but got no stomach ache.
        If nostalgia is the metaphor I fling out,

like a bird looking for its favorite tree
    or a man pissed because a town is dying,
        then I am guilty for why Bristol's freight

and factory, fire and steam vanished.
    Unless God and the devil stay lost in preoccupations;
        unless Burger King and vast malls of indifference spread

like kudzu and asphalt, I'll stop, shrug or look past
    the steel mill's shattered glass and flecked paint
        to warped crossties near Dairy Queen's parking lot

where lovers slip milkshakes from the same straw.
    Ten years ago I passed the mill's detritus: nuts and bolts,
        stuck in red clay, as black as the rotting fruit

fallen from a pignut hickory.
    It wasn't hard to picture Dad flagging a freight train,
        sooty sweat streaking his face,

the sucking slam down of fire bucket and drop forge,
    deafening behind the blistered walls—
        the lunch whistle I heard miles away,

even knee-deep in creek silt with my brother
    netting crayfish. But even memory rusts or grows,
        like a hickory sending down a taproot,

and if a man dies sooner than a town,
    not to speak of this is a kind of death.
        Dad chopped a shagbark hickory to burn

for smoked ham. And if I do not forget the thrush
    that flew with the first blow, white worms
        under the bark that fell and crawled with sawdust,

then this rings more than an elegy for trees that pushed
    leaves into soot and cindered air,
        into matches as I biked to streams that crossed

beneath trestles to swim naked, listen to water's small song
    across stones and downed limbs and sometimes forget
        who I was, ignore time as the sun

spread its stain beneath sycamore and willow,
    the air growing cool
        as stones at the bottom of the water

II.

SARTRE IN THE HAYLOFT

It's cooler here, reading about nothingness
      in the hay. I'm so far into the abstract heart
        of all that matters, my noodle soup
has grown as cold as rafter nails.
      I yawn, put the book aside. I love the chapter
        on relating to others, especially how
desire links closely to flesh—not that different
      from what my father said forty years ago
        when I complained about my girl friend
dropping me. "You ain't shit
      unless somebody says you're shit."
        The cat that followed me up here
flicks her ears. Mourning doves coo from the lightning rod.
      A crow chases them away.
        I picture my wife, untouched by me all night.
I shiver. The book hasn't told me anything
      a crow can't, sometimes shaking rain
        into its shadow before claiming dumpster secrets.
I'm hungry, and if I left the TV on,
      depending on her mood, my wife might be pissed.
        Since I exist for the other,
I grab the book and hurry down
      the ladder toward first light.

DRIVING PAST CHERRY HILL

From a bowling ball and shoe polish
factory, oily wind smells. Near Cherry Hill
I take a right past a kennel
and a gas station.

Sometimes a few miles from home, I swing up
a gravel road leading to an abandoned farm house.
Broken windows, beer cans. I kill the engine
and turn up Coltrane or Mingus and think
does a rhythm pulse between millions of stars
and crickets turned to the evening's chill?

I snap open a beer, flip open a journal.
The stars look hammered in place,
bright as newly-forged hammer heads.
Opening the door, I silence the crickets.
I try to move a few words toward music
but I fail, like the air around me fails.

And the rusted wrecks, some draped with vines,
aren't doing any better. But in a few months
those vines may push out flowers.
From the fence something winged
calls *two-weet*. Not a love song.
Then quiet. First light breaks through
cracks in the fence. A red-winged blackbird
is looking my way. There is a great
distance between love and silence.

ORPHEUS BUYS A HARLEY

"I want a black one. No extra chrome or lights,
just what's legal. Day or night,
I don't want to be too obvious and no mirrors.
I'll hand signal and look over my shoulder."
The shop owner's thinking he's nuts or something,
but the wad of U.S. Grants eases all
considerations. "Most importantly," Orpheus says,
"If you can outfit a 900 with small, bird-like
whistles, I'd be happy. Put'em on the wheels
and handlebars. The faster I go the louder
the whistling, as though the blacktop and I become
one blurred, high-pitched song spinning back
to the gods. Know what I mean?"
The clerk nods. "You must think I'm full of shit,
but I hope you can do it."
The man smiles as Orpheus unrolls the bills.
"So it's a deal. Don't forget, no mirror.
I don't care how you do it, just don't scar
the paint; mirrors are for beginners or paranoids."

THE MUSE'S FIST

A bruise on the lake—I mean the water.
A bruised flea. The one on my dog's neck.
A cosmic bruise, like a star yelping. Stars only evoke feelings.
Bruised nerves, not to be confused with a lover's refusal.
A bruised house. No hailstones, etc. We're talking
messed-up silence.
A bruised girl dying in a diabetic coma,
though prayers are lifted up.
A bruised sofa, not to forget moans sinking in the stained fabric.
A bruised book and the muse's fingerprints on the dog ears.
A bruised nail that won't draw hammer sparks on the barn.
A bruised dog, or its misused brain, who will fight to kill.
A bruise where pines touch a swamp near a still and a motor court.
A bruise where time runs around, its head severed, and screams are
mistaken for songs. A bruise, deep and painful,
that turns purple, blue, green, and refuses to leave.

BRUISES

Bruised songs. Karaoke does that.
Bruised rain. You mean the way
gasoline in a puddle changes the water
to red or green and all washes away.
Bruised cigarette. You mean a torn one.
Bruised robot singing. But wouldn't
the metal skin simply dent?
Bruised hospital. The one with piss odors
and homeless in the hallway and a mop bucket
by the nurses' station, where the cab
took you when your heart ticked wrong.
Bruised tattoo, where I squeezed you
too hard on your arm because, desperate,
I wanted you to live. Bruised feathers,
bruised doughnuts in coffee, the way
I saw the night flowers when we left
Emergency, wanting some blues
in the bruised darkness.

POET FOR HIRE

Disappointed with reality? Rent a poet.
Watch the sun burn his back as the poet
mows your lawn, and the grass, no poet
would track inside, blooms in his hands:
a bouquet. He's blinking salt-sweat
in his eyes, for you, not from desire but how a poet
sees a word, like blade or grass, oil or rent
sharpening his tongue on all that. Any poet,
thirsty and tired, would call water something
rented lips touch, aching to swallow.
The poem may not be handsome nor you
beautiful but given time, pen and paper,
a dream you may have of transport,
or the new moon past a hummingbird
needling a passionflower can be yours.

SNAKE PANTOUM

Snakes that live near the swamp
become dead skin at road's edge
or weave into fallen petals, leaves, mud;
shift in moonlight into talismans,

become live wires in children's hands
at road's edge or wood's heart;
shift in moonlight into talismans
you put faith in or not, head bowed

at road's edge or wood's heart,
where you, snake-driven, hunt or not.
You put faith in them, head bowed or not—
copperhead, rattler, water moccasin,

where you, snake-driven, hunt or not,
pray over a live snake or mourn a dead one—
copperhead, rattler, water moccasin: serpents
that tell you what you are or will be

as you pray over a live diamondback or mourn for
yourself in moss, ferns or piled pine needles
that tell you what you are or will be,
stooping, stumbling or crawling in musty dark

where snakes may curl, hiss and weave
into fallen leaves, petals, mud,
not caring who you are, yet wary, not your charm—
snakes that live near the swamp.

NIGHT SHIFT AT THE TEDDY BEAR FACTORY

I cart parts—velveteen, ribbons, polyester
stuffing—to the lines manned by women who wear
masks, since the bears come inside-out,
seams exposed, openings down the back.
Some of the assemblers pedal sewing machines,
adding eyes and grommet attachments to each face,
then stitch the parts together.

Some of the women dislike my walking around
down-time. Someone told Sue, the super,
so I spend more time in the supply room,
reading Plato, sighing at the moral perfection
he wanted, the "good life" reigning.
I catch snippets: Mary Jean tells Tammi how she'd
trade her man for Kevin on *The Guiding Light*

while I sweep up, sometimes a half-finished or
damaged bear: someone turned the air pressure
too high on the stuffing machine that blows in
the fluff through a narrow tube; or the "bear surgeon"
at the end of the line, hanging on a country tune
twanging from the radio, missed a stitch
up the spinal slit.

I toss the aborted teddies in the trash.
And the best part: when I slip Paula a stay-awake pill,
then sit with her at break as she bitches about Dave,
who sleeps half the day, won't work, leaves beer cans
and muddy biker boots in the bathroom...
Tapping her finger, as I did
last night, I tap again.

DID KAFKA EVER DROP A FAILED STORY

into the trash at work?
Say he knew the janitor might see it – a story
about a janitor who sees the woman who
leaves the odor of lemons in her office
and won't say she loves him when he stands
beside her desk and tries to hand her roses.

One day he walks to her office to spy on her.
She is chewing out someone on the phone.
A vase of violets sits on her right.
She hangs up as he pretends to read
by the coat rack. He imagined her blonde
but her hair is as black as a phone.

He turns and leaves. That night he touches
her chair, wipes lipstick from the phone
with his shirttail. What can he do
but inhale, close his eyes, see her
but never know her, just know
the lemony veil that haunts the room.

RETIREMENT MATTERS

What mattered: bulging wallets,
like cabbages in our garden.
What mattered: love on sweaty
nights, lemonade, TV ... Now, TV
flattens thin plots thinner, so I drift
into a magazine article, which tries
to explain lust. What matters is you
as we hold each other between
tragedies: someone on a jet
lights a fuse in his sock.
Someone down the block
knocks his daughter's teeth loose.

What matters: you lean toward your
asters while I wander a railroad track—
plum, cherry, hawthorn past barbed wire—
blossomed perfume hovering
beneath the moon. Sometimes I brush
against pine needles or red sumac,
even picture myself as a flying squirrel
or a jack-hammering wood pecker.

Sometimes an owl or a hawk
cracks a limb overhead. What cracks
in the heart is never stocks or bonds
but what to say: to say it right, rhythm
and tone exact—same as the top wire
of our fence, still shiny after years,
where you drop popcorn and bread crusts
near the feeder for starlings and blue jays
while goldfinch and warblers wait, and we,
behind the door's window, point and hold.

ANATOMY 101

The skeleton's missing two knuckles. Lecture
droning. I'd rather shoot an imaginary pitch
pine up a hundred feet.
Did he work at a sawmill and drink himself
down to the bone at clip joints? And maybe more tragic,
how did his wife convince the mortician to soak
the corpse in acid, leaving the bones
she'd sell to a skeleton business?

The chain of bones, tagged and numbered,
clinks. Dust rises and falls. Hour waning,
the shadow down the board to the floor,
harp of bones on hardwood.
I need to know knuckles, tiny wires
holding the rest. Were the knuckles jostled
in transit, gnawed by some animal,
stolen by someone who wears them around his neck?

Did the model wear a ruby ring, emerald,
maybe even a hammered dime
circling a missing half digit?
At the mill, did he turn one noon
to his wife who brought his tuna sandwich
and apple because he forgot them?
Caught up by her perfume, one hand
still touching the log, blade whining
toward bones, rings, you name it.

RUNNING BACKWARDS

Reading about a dog lifting his paw,
meaning yes, to questions about hopes for joy
and riches for passersby, I know the tale
gets tricky. Money, jewelry, Mercedes whir
like a film running backwards to…to Stop, there,
I had no worries: a child, ice cream dribbling down the chin,
sits on the porch steps, setter asleep on the stoop.
Mother's in her sewing room pedaling her Singer.
Sister leans back in the swing, nipples firm
against a yellow halter, as she watches low-slung cars
drift by—duck-tailed boys who might
offer her beer and lies form some happiness.
A garden spider crouches in the dead center
of its web between two hollyhocks,
nowhere near a metaphor for joy.

SILAGE

You roll up the windows and still
your eyes water. Hay, alfalfa,
cornstalks, up and down the silo—
drip drip and black rot, then fodder.

Look at the cows, look at the house,
lightning rods above the attic's blue
shutters. Look at the man on a tractor,
his green and yellow cap. Green on his boots,
green under his fingernails.

Here come his kids off the school bus.
A boy and girl, 12 and 13. They saw a film
about sex today—no faces, just body parts.
Someone whispered "It'll make you close your eyes."

The boy must cut firewood and bring in
the cows before he can play baseball.
After the green drips long into fall and winter
when the tractor backs up to the silo,

the stink then socks the lungs, clears his head
as he works a pitchfork, geometry and baseball
fusing in a dream of a curve ball
he knocks over the charged fence.

Before sleep the girl pictures some actress' face
and wonders how her body moved in the movie.
Words the teacher muttered –*vas deferens,
fallopian tubes* – hung as heavy on the class
as looks the boys gave the girls.

And if the girl remembers her dreams
sex may or may not show—one stalk
working its way into another
inside the silver tip under the stars
she can see from her window.

TOBACCO

You can't use the words *infinity* and *eternity* in the same poem.
—Josh Grimes

Bending, slashing, staking leaves on poles that Bobby Joe
and I carted to the barn to hang on racks to cure,
I didn't think of an infinity of anything,
unless the infinite sun licking my neck made me swear
and rise to swipe my face with my bandana.
At noon we broke for mashed potatoes, gravy,
pork chops, pitcher of milk, biscuits thick as yo-yos—
cherry pie so rich, fruit dribbled over the sides.
One of the farmer's daughters wore a wine-colored T-shirt,
straw-colored hair hanging down her back.
I skipped dessert; cutting rows sleepy wouldn't work.

We cut toward the well so we could drink
every fifteen minutes or so.
I didn't know the juice, color of cider, would stick
and clump on my hands and wrists. Bobby Joe
hadn't told me about gloves. An astringent, the juice
pulled poisons straight from my pores.
Rising to wipe my neck, I saw the girl hanging wash
about forty yards away. Bras and panties—pastel blue,
green, red—sunlight filling each stitched curve with gold.
The girl stooped to pick more laundry. The back of her jeans
stretched tight as the blue map flat on my bedroom wall.

She stood and her breasts jostled, as if
kittens wanted to free themselves. I fell behind,
sighing, probably saying something like, "Bobby Joe,
look at that. What beauty." Mad because his dad
had lined up this job, he just said, "You're falling behind.
We've got till eight and are getting paid by the cart-load.
Old Jackson'll know how many carts."
Later I washed the tobacco off with Lava.
Felt ten pounds lighter. We stood by a cart and faced the moon.

The girl flicked on her bedroom light.
I'd be lying if I said I didn't want her to undress.

She sat down at a desk and began typing,
perhaps struggling with an essay or a poem.
I pictured Sandra Dee in *A Summer Place*.
When she and Troy Donahue kissed, and in later scenes,
If they said, I'll love you forever," eternity was
palpable, and whether life is for happiness or not,
I would never see that girl again.

THE KNIFE-THROWER'S LADY

Never raised you for that,
says her mother's cruise ship trip postcard.
Right, but the man who throws knives at her
spinning body at the sideshow and the men
she screws for money pay her well.

Sometimes she hears, as the blades twirl,
"Who will save her if she gets one in the heart?"
They seem to feel, she thinks, that something
about her will save some part of them.
It's the same feeling she gets from the men

who pray to her toenails or the one who wept
and pled, "Oh Mary, mother of Jesus,
whip me with your hair." And since her hair
falls down her back, she flogged his face
until his drool wet the blonde tips.

She wants to say I can't save anyone;
not the peg-legged man who sweeps up
after the show; not the woman upstairs
in my hotel, who plays Patsy Cline
too loud on a stereo; and surely not Margo,

ticket-taker, blue spiked hair,
no bra, and wants her, she says—
would kill to have her.
Save them from what? Maybe they don't want
to be saved. Maybe their souls aren't worth

a panhandler's dime. They were raised the way
they were raised: to throw the knife or take it;
to give in or hold court; to buy or sell;
to say Damn, that's good--or say grace
as the body's seeds spark in the dark.

And sometimes the knife thrower, on encore,
will lower the lights, set the blades afire,

and nothing, as the daggers fly, but the sequins
on tights glow, petals of fire growing one
by one around her body.

III.

SOUL

Charlie "Bird" Parker (1921-1955)

I don't remember the name of the club,
a smoky place, wobbly tables, scarred stage,
torn purple curtain. "Blowing his goddamn
heart out, "said the woman beside me.
I thought Bird strained, notes getting tighter,
toward improvised bliss. But what did I know?
"He's got more soul than this whole place,"
the woman said. The music lifted Bird,
made his instrument a part of him, lips to heart
and below. He was blowing everything into that horn:
art history, current events, stone age culture…
Then a rat ran behind him at the edge
of the curtain and disappeared. No one
stirred. Was I the only one who saw it?
Music freezes time, that linear root
that nails the soul to earth.
Maybe the crowd froze in time as Bird
blew the blues across us—the rat
somewhere in its own bluesy world.
Bird finished and came down to our table.
The woman handed him her cigarette
and introduced me. Bird mentioned
his visit to the Modern Art Museum
and asked if I had seen the Degas show.
Those ballerinas looked so other-worldly,
suspended in red, blue, green back-light.
I hadn't and I wanted to say something clever
about the rat scampering from the music,
but Bird ignored me and began to stroke
the woman's hand. Soul, that light in the smoke,
floated across the room, on Bird's eyebrow sweat,
in the knuckled blood under the woman's ring
finger, and the peanut-sized heart of the rat—
a few seconds of "Confirmation" down its delicate
ears wherever it was, caught between music
and noise, the 2-4 start of drums again

and the perfect knowing—the heart pumping
and letting it in simultaneously.

—for Michael Waters

SUN IN AN EMPTY ROOM

after Edward Hopper

You could say the sunlight
shining through the window
aches to fill the room or just
wants to be there, but that
would be pushing it. Far from us
the light needs no human presence
to flesh out its meaning. No body,
visible past the shadows,
gives the light an edge as it,
broken by a recessed wall, falls twice
on the dull floor, and the light's shadows,
gray as gravestones, soften the wall paper.

Maybe the light holds a story,
since some leaves, elm or birch,
show at one side of the window.
A grove of trees, or the edge
of a forest, it's hard to tell.
The unwritten story could interest
anyone, a tale with no apparent
characters, no defined plot.
What can you say? The light
casts dominion. Dust, bright as sugar,
rises, falls. Something is clear
and final. Maybe someone in bed with
someone on the far side of the room
says, "Look, the light falls
beautifully on the floor."

ARTISTS AND TREES—MT. SAN ANGELO

They paint shadows near a hemlock,
moss speckling the far side of an oak—
and capture the copper beech
lightning split, its amputated firewood,
leafless, scarred timber.
And they'll paint mockingbird, blue jay, finch,
sparrow claiming black willow, pecan,
gingko, so close to their leaves almost touch,
the way lovers round off the scene in movies,
serious words whispered, leaves almost brushing
their hair, sweethearts hardly knowing they lean
against bark—the way it should be—
the silence, the rings, the years, letting go.

THOREAU'S HEMORRHOIDS

Maybe he put a nail in his onion
and potato soup once too often,
or ate beef a bit undercooked for years.
Maybe he blamed all of it on God,
or maybe the thought of God was the ice
fanned into feathery swirls on his bedroom window,
and cold at night he hated the icy beauty
but still loved God.

I was teaching *Walden* to freshmen,
and most of them thought Thoreau
an eccentric loner and somewhat of an elitist.
A learned man practicing his friend Emerson's
self-reliance and criticizing society's bullshit
and the rusty nails it kept hammering
into the crate-shape coffin
he knew how to saw and hammer for himself.

Picture him, insomniac and no woman
to rub his back, aching from stacking chopped wood.
He sits up nights, sipping tea and reading
parts of the Bible that spurred Whitman.
He'll glance at the moon, that frozen candle
that blurs the fragile ice
but lights everything he thinks about.

THE MAD BOMBER DREAMING
HE'S HENRY DAVID THOREAU

Where's my sink and where's my refrigerator?
Why is that journal on my footstool?
A line on a page reads *Praise the bean vines*
as you praise the far stars. Did I write that?
Where's my bomb works? Boxes, powder,
wicks, wires? I don't get it. I feel calm,
real calm. I'm worrying about enough nails
for a fence, want to hoe a field,

check for rabbit damage to some greens.
Through the window I see strawberry,
johnswort, sand cherry and ground nut
filling the yard, but I don't recall seeing them
yesterday. I heard a cowbird call back
to a phoebe, sounding like odd bells rung
at intervals. Don't I feel indifferent to birds and hate
people, especially those who misunderstand me.

A jar labeled herbal tea on the table.
I don't drink tea. Damn, that's my handwriting
in the book. I don't see one thing that's mine,
not even wrapping paper and stamps to mail
my good wishes. How far must a man go
to know who he is? Did I write these words?
When you're planting seeds, stick your hand
into the soft earth all the way
to your wrist and you will know.

SHOULD THE MOON

Let's say the moon can't see the tongues
of lovers licking each other's neck
as they lean against a fence by a silo.
Let's say the moon is blind. Of course it is.
It's not human, even though it affects tides.
Let's say tether of light, tether of gravity.
Let's say the moon isn't kind. Of course, it isn't;
see line five. It enforces its own curfew,
and the different hats it wears are, more or less,
shadows. How much of the moon can you
stomach? Victim or cruel one in songs,
the moon rolls on. Let's say bald doll, where age
is no factor. Let's say ice along the road, and scorched
shingles on an abandoned farm house the moon
lights up. Let's say I find the diary of a girl
named Diane in a dresser drawer. A poem
every few pages, a moon in nearly every poem.
And I'll say this: the word *love*
stands in every corner,
naked, or floats above the bed—
the moon over its shoulder.

DESERT SNOW

It's almost Christmas. I stand beside a saguaro.
I don't know if God had anything to do
with this cactus, but the backward-curving
branches, the white flowers and edible
red fruit remind me of an oasis.

First stars tonight, and they give me faith,
not in their fire but in their light,
which once lit up a cacomistle.
Desert squirrel, I thought, but they don't swish
a black-banded tail.

Last night I watched a woman
at a cantina dance the cachucha, alone,
but a cacophony of vultures interrupts
that image. Something must be dead
in the arroyo, but as I bite into this fruit,

I don't care about anything dead.
Strings of lights, even on adobe shacks
near the desert, are the only decorations.
I have little faith on snow falling on the desert,
but some would love a white Christmas.

for Donald Revell

LORCA IN NEW YORK

He endured a streetlight subway
transformation: no blood moon
over the wash between fire escapes,
no rooster crowing in the shipyard.

He saw gasoline rainbows near the curbs,
condom flowers, poor whores huddled in the orchard
behind a bakery—three apple trees, actually,
among car tires and paint cans.

Lorca worried about women in the dirty rain,
their ratty hair, holes in dresses.
He ordered eggs over easy, eavesdropped on two
longshoremen talking about bookies.

Lorca wondered why New York sunsets
looked so hazy. Then he rubbed some sulfur
from his eyes. He hated guns, rarely wrote
about that, even hated the sight of guns.

He wondered why Whitman had so much faith
in America: these prostitutes, gamblers, con-
artists…, this New York and its beggars and drunks.
Lorca, with his brief but furious hope: at night

Brooklyn Bridge lit like a steel chandelier—
black river, barges of salt and rubber.
Stoplight halos, perfumed, predatory creatures.
Beautiful heart, beautiful heart, beautiful heart.

AN UN-PRAYED-FOR SONG

What was the greenhouse? It
was a jungle, and it was a
paradise, it was order and
disorder: Was it an escape?
No, for it was a reality
harsher than reality.

—Theodore Roethke

Whipped for daydreaming he retreated to his closet
and became wedded to the magnet of darkness
but always fought the pull clear to his bones;
always looked for a hair of light in anything,
especially behind the hot glass where he watered
flowers, and eyed steam gauges with such intensity
in winter, he forgot his bruised buttocks.

Those fragile stems that bleed at a touch,
petals that wilt from a cough didn't talk back,
didn't tell dirty jokes or doubt his stories from sleep
about a child who rode a swan toward a sun-
drenched horizon and beyond to the stars.
He raked spilled manure and dead seeds for birds:
sparrows, blackbirds, scarlet tanagers, blue jays…

From examining the wreckage of a blackbird
his father shot, he knew that deep in the craw
is a bone the precise length and sharpness of a needle;
and the transparent skull must vibrate to
each song like the skin of the thinnest drum.
His sons behind the double-glass of bone meal,
mist and prize roses weren't Dorsey, but for

blossoms in the flesh; to offset the whippings
when the scum and lime thickened and unborn
songs grew, nourished like accusing
chrysanthemums. Within the loam and seed
of each song was the question of forgiving his father.

If the boy's words kissed the mouth of a bat,
it was his mother. If the ghost of a bluegill
floundered in the soggy water, it was his father.

But the forgiveness always swam in the dark
bones beneath his songs of the flesh.
He painted his words on the glass helmet of his soul.
Years later, drunk, he chided the genius literati,
broke an ottoman across a table and pounded out
windows with his fist. Stretched under a pool table

or rolling in a meadow of violets, he measured
rhythms the way he packed the greenhouse dirt
in flower boxes. Crying in a closet the same way
he did as a child, he wondered if it's the poet's
business to remember, God's to forgive.
When he quit therapy, a flower surfaced,
pressed like the star of a sand dollar on the temporal bone

tucked under and behind the brain. How little time
he had to forgive himself when faces were
crying in his dreams for forgiveness. And a few
were singing from earthy closets, new songs he had
prepared. Perhaps one rose, half finished in a dream,
a sick old man who, like a child,
needs stories or songs and is already surrounded by

funereal perfume. Perhaps he was teasing words
while he lounged in a pool, breaking rhymes toward
order, moving them around like a lawnmower
sparking stones, then his heart catching
like a trout on a hook, he swallowed the words: fish
sun, forgiveness…and all chances for songs
of anguish or joy in the skin-puckering water.

WITTGENSTEIN'S HUT

Grasshoppers click in the creepers like fast
clocks. I could care less about time.
Even 3 times 7 equals 21 is as abstract
as the shape and color of wind
through needles around pink thistle
where a bumblebee patrols.
I'm a stumblebum on the way to something
I must give up: love? Myself?
The rational beauty of the real world?

Wait. What is the logic of a fox
digging at chicken bones I threw out?
Eyes on fire in the dark, past hunger,
much different than the passion I felt
building my first sewing machine.
Gears, wheels, the oily mathematics of this loop
to the flywheel kept me from games, girls,
even the sunshine through the lindens.

The sky in the east glows red as sumac,
but in the west it looks like rain.
A drizzle, I hope – the hut leaks – down
through nests and needles, darkening
the deer's and fox's backs as they grow wet.
The tiny stove is never enough.
I'll build a brush fire if it doesn't
rain long. I love to feel a fire take the blue
steel out of wind. Nights being counted
with a sense of care rather than of order.

VIABLE TWIGS

A.R. Ammons (1926-2001)

I had to shift sideways, inhale the odor
of old sofas and bleached paper
beneath the sign: *Watch for Falling*
Books before I found the *Collected 1951-1977.*
The inside page, scissored to a jagged edge—
blue stamped ink: *Withdrawn from the Library.*
I flipped to "Viable" caught the movements of redbird,
robin, and worm—the chain showing its dangerous links,
its beautiful sounders of hunger and execution—
no less the cardinal among cherry blossoms in Tennessee,
1959, that started in an invisible place,
hung an earring on each twig, then fell.
Even when I climbed the black cherry boughs
in the alley behind Zeke's Body Shop,
bruising the fruit in my urgency,
I knew each naked twig blossomed and went
naked again between cherries when the leaves fell,
but I didn't know what that meant, exactly.

GULLS ABOVE PRISON WALLS

—Denise Levertov (1923-1998)

An inmate wrote to me that he discovered your poem
about the vulva not to be stared at,
which confused him, since he heard Annie Sprinkle
let people for art spy hers up close.

He wants more of your gulls in gray arcs,
more precise longings for love to transcend human
failings—more unfastening of leaf
from stem and brief descent.

He'll gladly embrace poems to fill the absence
that mounts like blocks, dark squares, hard and cold.
I'm sending him more of your hopeful clarity,
disguised as gulls ascending heavenward,

to float your death,
ease the dread and silence.

MY MACHO DOUBLE

after John Ashbery

Unlike your double, mine likes to work.
He once wore a "wire" in a leather bar
to check on a cheater. My double's blue
silk vest almost gave him away.
He swallowed a fishhook just to show
he could spit it up, no blood.
That, I think, was a dream.
He works here, shearing hedges
around a garden of asters and lilies.
I love flowers, especially bouquets,
but my double sometimes throws flowers
into the fireplace just to watch
the petals sear and shrink.

I don't trust my double.
He says that I love words too much.
He thinks he's sexy, wants me to dress
in flashy shirts, maybe even wants me.
Unlike your double, I don't think mine's
erotic. I have to keep an eye on him,
even when I'm eating ice cream.
My double wants that ice cream to become
a chocolate hand to caress my throat.
When he's traveling, I can walk and admire
blossoms and not think of the sky
as a filter between here and infinity.
The last time I told my double I loved words,
he flinched. I'm going to keep writing
until he retires to Tahiti or flops face down
on a barge of ice on one of his Kodak polar tours.

MARILYN MONROE TO ARTHUR RIMBAUD

So at seventeen you sent poems out.
Well, I always pressed my dresses perfectly
and loved the way my rear curved on the piano bench,
    and I won a recital at nine.
I'm not sure I understand you that much.
In your "Childhood" piece, are you hiding behind
    flowers, rainbows, gardens?
I think you're afraid of nudity, and that bothers me. And you say
you might be an abandoned child. I was.
    Who was my father? My mother labored in a lab,
cutting negative film: boring, tedious, blinding.
She dated many bad men, and later
    suffered a nervous breakdown,
called, by doctors, paranoid schizophrenia--
her end of the world. Arthur, were you too young
    to know when you pointed to your own break with reality?
Yet maybe you summoned it to remind yourself of it
and held it at bay, the way such heavy beauty
    overcame you, until you pulled crystal
waterfalls into your eyes, embraced whole fields of phlox
and buttercups. But for me, Arthur, everything is personal.
    You seem a step removed from real animals, even.
I've always loved them, especially since
some neighbor shot my dog, Tippy, when I was seven.
    And you, Arthur, you invented visions
to replace the painful bullshit. "Prairies of Love"—
yeah, sure. Let's dream on it.
    But I guess that got you through some dark days.
My dreams often wake me, sweating or shivering.
When they took my mother to a sanitarium,
    I went to a children's home.
Sometimes I slept with a pillow over my head.
Sometimes I stabbed my beef or pork at dinner,
    and the fork went *ting* on the plate.
I found a small frog in the fenced woods out back,
put it inside a box, poked holes in the lid and hid it
    under my bed. I poured water in a soda bottle cap.
I put in crickets, worms, nursing that frog,

loving it. Then one morning I opened the lid
and the frog lay on its back, feet
outstretched, stiff as a strip of leather--a cricket
In the corner, silent but not dead. Wasn't the frog
supposed to eat the cricket? Well, Arthur,
like you at the end, the frog was rotting, and like you,
the cricket was not budging, silent. And for what,
Arthur, for what?

RICHARD HUGO WON'T BE APPEARING TONIGHT

He didn't show in my dream last night,
hand around a glass of bourbon,
cigarette ash flecking his shirt.
He didn't mention trout fishing
in the Duwamish, a wine and cheese lunch.
He didn't say most bars are smoky graves,
a warm jukebox on a cold night.
He didn't point to pigeons and rats
not loving us for good reason.

He didn't say near copper mines
skunks and raccoons look ragged
because of damaged streams; didn't mention
our supply of sanity being nibbled away,
and though we check, the silo's
always near overflow.
He didn't tell me, though I may have believed him,
a fanatic bruising his knees in church
thinks the moon has been kidnapped,
and snow is plotting to overthrow the state.

Barn owls drifting from loft to vane
past dusk are assassins.
He didn't say anything about driving
half the night, spotting a diner
and telling a sunken-eyed waitress
"I love you" to make her feel better.
He didn't say one word about river bottoms
being places of resolution,
that the sun might rise on the fish market
and fruit stand of any cruel day.

He didn't say that the happiest time
is finding a creek past evergreens,
your line perfect for trout—
blue sky, no thoughts of money or women.
He lets the rhythm of the line do the talking.
Faint sounds: a great blue heron

or a hawk overhead, everything else
is quiet as the stones under his boots.

DARK ROAST

for Lynda Hull (1954-1994)

Was a poem percolating as she raced
the roads hiding black ice? Was she
dropping private tears so that what hurt her
was as removed as a dusty hearse
in some vine-draped garage?

The crash scarred a maple
that took months to heal
and left a mark the color of her hair.

Recycled metal, her car may be the coffee can
you open one morning, and the whoosh
of the popped vacuum is, as she might put it,
what a poem finished does – and you remember dark
roast, with a sprig of chicory, her favorite.

IV.

WORDS NEVER SAID

My student wrote *star smoke, star love, star cape…*
into poem after poem and told me once that her father
never said he loved her, but bought her dolls,
drove her to school and tucked her in
each night with a kiss.

Experts say we need to hear the words, but what if
they aren't true? What if someone cannot say
the right thing at the right time
because someone beat him
for not slopping the pigs?

What if someone got sworn at for painting her nails
carnal red? Doesn't the Bible rig the game,
making it hard to be human?
Sissies don't cry. Buck up,
make good grades

and you can have a car….
My student drove her car
into an oak off the roadside.
I don't know if her father cried at her funeral.
I asked my student once why so many stars

in her poems? *They make the dark beautiful,*
she said. *When they die they tend to shrink*
in an odd way, sucking everything in.
It's all delicious energy whirling—
then she danced out of the room.

WHEN THE MIRACULOUS DOESN'T HAPPEN

My oldest student, who shares
two children with her ex
and works in a nursing home,
knows why Nora had to leave
her children, her doll life and walk
into Oslo's dark, snowy streets —
and, like Nora, knows how love,
like bon-bons, looks sweet, grows stale,
and then something devours it.

My youngest student, basketball
player, struggling with drama,
doesn't think Nora understands Torvald,
that the business world
can chew you up.
Another student, who drags her guitar
to class (she plays on the street for money)
wrote on a quiz. "Nora doesn't want to lie
in that coffin-shaped bed anymore."

I'm taking Nora a step away from the play.
Walking a long way, Nora feels
blisters on her heels. In her coat pocket
she touches her daughter's hairbrush —
feels some hairs, thin, soft, like angel-hair
on their Christmas tree. A gray dog,
rib-bones showing, sniffs Nora's ankles.
Winter birds, voiceless, leap like
asterisks, branch to branch, in a bare tree.

Does Nora see them? Something many
of my students don't quite see
disturbs them. The silence, the snow,
the silence, the snow.

FLUCTUATIONS

If you're high enough in office,
        an irregular heartbeat
                can stir the stock market.

Nationwide, frogs are dying
        at an alarming rate. Some turn
                into zombies first.

This bobwhite outside interrupts everything
        I try to get down. Oh well,
                Bobwhite, bobwhite…

If you're low enough, you get blamed
        for stealing letters, checks, or you catch
                government thieves and become a hero.

In between, new pain medication hits
        the market. Return to exercise slowly,
                watch arthritis in hips and knees.

Use machines. A bobwhite's heart, a Japanese
        millionaire's, a frog dozing on a log
                in the Everglades depend on it.

IN A DARK TIME THE EYE
after Theodore Roethke

begins to see clouds, a lake, shit
the president slings day and night,
or none of the above?
In a dark time cowboy boots shine,
barbells rise, barbecue smoke curls.
No gay clouds, no sodomy in the Bible zone,
or some of the above?

In a dark time summer thunderheads, stacked
like purple plates, break to lightning.
Hail drills down, marble-sized, and all
of the above percolate down each blade of grass
and fills potholes the city won't patch.
What god gives us each scene, lets us
develop it behind our eyes?

Not so far from here clouds shade the lake,
fish dart between rocks.
The Vaseline factory flushes yellow matter
into the river that links two lakes.
I'm grinding coffee while a cardinal turns
our black clothesline white. He's singing,
as if he's all that matters.

GOD AND THE WINDSHIELD WASHER

(Baltimore, 1999)

God slips through droppings a pigeon
leaves behind peanut shells
as a cop jerks a boy away from a car,
stopped at the light—a boy with a rag in one hand
and a bottle of blue liquid in the other.
The cop grabs the boy's ear
and he, cursing, grows soft in the knees.
Taking a step toward them, I can't tell if
the boy is back-talking, won't drop his gear
or wants to defend himself.
He crumbles to his knees, reaches toward
his back pocket, then hands over his wallet.
The cop slams the wallet toward the kid's chin,
picks up the rags and Windex and goes.
The boy sticks up a finger, God on the nail.
The boy catches my look, my hand rising.
He starts to raise his hand but stops
and glares, as though I'm making fun of him.

Maybe God plans to visit the boy
to straighten him on how to watch for
cops, get to the driver's side quicker
and squirt soap before the driver
opens his mouth, betting a good number
will fork over a dollar. The boy will learn
many corners with long lights, few cops,
even though it's not illegal to ask to clean
windshields, no more than "shine man?"
And God's only an image as I imagine
that boy wiping fast, nine degrees,
suds starting to freeze and streak,
fewer windows rolling down.
God hangs on the rag's unraveling threads,
stares through the white around the boy's dark
eyes, rooted in the veins running,
crossing into ganglia and an abstract spot

where a little hope dwells, where love
and shit get mixed up, where things happen
for no reason in the filthy air.

BEAUTIFUL RIVER, DIRTY WATER

for James Wright

The Ohio River, color of wash water,
flows fast past Portsmouth—crack pipes
on the bank, some probably on the bottom.

A man, whose vices are cigarettes and alcohol,
parks at the shoelace factory, closed
for years, and stares toward the broken windows,

litter, and a blue rag the wind
has shoved against a bald tire.
He opens the glove box, glances at a pistol

that could end it all, but then thinks of his wife,
pregnant, who swishes away from truckers,
who comment on her ass at the Pine Cone.

He thinks of deer season, how he loves to take
the perfect shot, and after field dressing,
how reaching in and gripping the wet guts,

steam rising, no longer bothers him.
How he loves to wait and smoke and bullshit
while the butcher prepares the meat;

how he like to try something new, like wrapping
some of the venison in bacon and onion
before roasting the tenderloin.

And tonight, his one headlight
illuminating the blue rag and tire,
he hears some pigeons and feels like

throwing a rock at a window.
The moon looks like the inside
of a chipped china cup, like the one

he sometimes gets at Pine Cone.
He grits his teeth, wonders if he should
carry a gun, watching his wife

take the truckers' shit,
because the wider her smile, the larger the tip.

BREAKFAST AND DOG WALK

It's my son's toy train wrecked on the carpet,
and his whining. It's the aspirin for my heart
and the anti-anxiety drugs, and how my inner life,
such as it is, is a pan of simmering bacon,
a blue jay hogging seeds while sparrows
fidget in the grass, and that's just *this* morning.
But I can walk my dog in the snow
and declare a maple with no hat is beautiful.
What do dead leaves symbolize besides death?
A cold stove is out of order in a room full of
clucking chickens, but why would chickens be there?

Aren't ideas, with no ham or beef on the bones,
dangerous and make the inner life sluggish and dull?
But someone loves the spotlight on the ice cream factory.
Someone loves the dinosaurs that chased humans
but won't write about it—his brain, satisfied.
I lift dog turds from the snow, almost fall
in love with a quiet weathervane.
All this paying attention to my dog's loose chain,
street signs, parked trucks, my neighbor's blue ice sculptures,
a scarred red boat in a driveway—
all of it hard to deal with, even harder to define.

SUZI'S TEDDY BEAR

On my hike a drizzle starts,
so I shortcut through a graveyard.
I stop to take a breath,
a tan teddy, size of a loaf of bread,
soggy, on the marble; Suzi Ames—Born June 11, 1989—
died July 7, 2000. Suzi, I'm claiming your wet bear
for all of us. His button eyes, stuffing dribbling
from his nose. Chewed left ear. Will those skunks
or squirrels ever learn? Was this your
favorite bear? Did you diaper him with the dolls?
I'm not being silly. My daughter diapered hers.
Did you get a chance to touch the nipple
of your small bottle to his lips?
Suzi, you won't read this, but that's something
rubbery one grave over. Some come here at night,
I guess, and touch their skin to granite or polished marble.
Something scary and loony, something wild
and wrong, many people say, but so is
disappearing at eleven. Suzi, I have no idea
where you are. Maybe starlight penetrates your
coffin, upsetting slugs and worms.
Let's say it does. You may not have known, barring
accident, what was happening to you.
Let's say we all need a teddy bear, even those
who screw around here. Let's say another bear
lies with you, touching your spine.
Let's say, teddy bears, millions of them,
live at the center of the universe, but gravity,
and a language they've yet to learn,
keeps them from getting what they want.

HOLIDAY

A barefoot woman, nude
bursts from a July 4th party next door,
and sprints across the lawn around 3:00 a.m.
I'm smoking a cigar, sitting
in my porch swing.
As she rounds a hedge, I think I see what
looks like the tattoo of a blue butterfly
above her ass cleft.
I'll give myself a quiz: 1) Was she about
to get raped, or was raped?
2) Was she about to shower (she lives there)
and a spider the size of a pin cushion
scrambled from behind the toilet—a severe
fear of spiders bolting her out of the house?
Fat chance with partiers there.
3) Were they playing "truth or dare"
and she took the dare—and the scream
topped off the whole charade?
She hasn't returned. Cigar smoked.
It's been seven minutes, and no one
has searched for her. Maybe I should add
4) Is she crazy? Crazy or not,
a nude in moonlight has plenty of
possibilities, most bad, the least of all
broken glass, stray dogs. But if some
horny drunk, from the party or not,
sees her coming, crazy and beautiful, then what?
Fuck those stupid partiers. I have
nothing better to do, so I round the hedge
and hurry my pace, a blanket
from the swing's back under one arm.

MAP OF THE ARCTIC AT THE AA MEETING

Smoking and talking non-stop,
he says, "When I try to keep two women's faces in my head,
I always drift toward cocktails. To calm down,
I dive into Berryman's *Dreamsongs*."
A young woman, ratted hair and cut-myself
scars on her wrists, says, "Who's Berryman?"
"Doesn't matter," he says, and she says, "Then why
mention him, smartass?"
It's situations like this that make life boring
and boorish, and I'm glad she implied that he was both.

By the time he's through talking, someone's waving
his smoke away. Why did someone thumb-tack a map
of the Arctic Ocean above the coffee urns?
The world's smallest ocean and least explored.
A drifting ice cap hiding oil.
I've been here several times and no one
has ever mentioned
the map, talked about seals, polar bears
or how fast the ice
is warming and changing beneath.

This isn't the right forum, but just once
I'd like to hear someone say, "Mental illness is
a metaphor." "I'm feeling sexy today." Or "What kind of person
shoots wolves from a helicopter?"
But no; we sit here, unlike Berryman and his fan,
not wanting to be in the world anymore.
We're making stopgap measures to stay, and always—
whether our hot air is helping to erode that crown
of ice or not—at the end, we hold hands
in a circle and say our prayers.

FICTIONAL DEVICES

In this story I'm the knife
someone, one night, for revenge,
plunges into a car tire.

In this plot I'm in control of bad
words that hurt to the point of crazy.
I'm the character who pops a flashbulb

in the face of someone bragging
about his sexual prowess
as he leans against a cypress.

In this story, forgive me, but my corrupt
nature is my only saving grace.
I say things like, *All you stupid*

fuckers don't understand a thing.
They know what I mean. Their jaws drop.
In this plot my eyes are leaves or pebbles.

I tend to drift or sit there, complicating things.
In this story I transcend clichés about unreliable
narrators, lessons learned, clear resolutions—

all because the men who understand
die a little every time they're with me,
but it feels good. At least, what's what they say.

I get lost in the rain, someone finds me,
I don't know why I exist and I can't change
a thing. That's why the stars impress me,

not to forget the way an octopus changes shape
and color, jetting ink as it swims from danger.
I'd like to hurt the asshole who screwed me.

I key his car. I'd like to steal a Picasso,
but my writer won't go there. I think

his first sentence is something like

As she stepped from the car, her skirt
hiked up, showing where her black hose ended.
I don't like that. And I'd tell him if I could.

I'd rather be sipping coffee at a truck stop,
sizing up snakeskin boots. Some guy wants to
show me his Peterbilt: CB radio,

Naugahyde seats. Maybe I'll say, "What's your handle?"
Maybe I'll run my hand across the faux leather,
purse my lips and step any way I want.

TELL ABOUT YOUR HAPPINESS AND YOUR SADNESS. TAKE AS LONG AS YOU LIKE.

after Mary Ruefle

My happiness slept in its own bed
and told my sadness to quit
wetting the pillow or it would leave.

My happiness baked biscuits while
my sadness sat in a corner, sulking,
then said, "You look like a ghost, a dumb ghost."

My happiness felt happy enough to lift the sky
on a mirror. My sadness pointed out that this
was scientifically impossible.

My happiness spotted a bird it didn't know
and clapped its hands. "You scared the bird away,"
said my sadness. "Get in the car, I'm hungry."

My happiness loves the red, pink, white April
flowers. My sadness would rather track in mud,
kick its shoes off and think nothing of it.

My happiness likes to dance rumba, tango,
samba, anything to make the blood tilt-a-whirl
along with the inexplicable thing that making

recurrent patterns on a floor to music does for the body
and more. My sadness would rather watch
lumberjacks on TV chop a block in-two.

My happiness thinks certain poems plant
something more precious than ore in the brain.
My sadness said, "I thought you said someone said,

Poetry makes nothing happen." "That was him,"
I said, "not my happiness."
My happiness likes to drink champagne,

take walks in rain or snow, and make love often.
My sadness doesn't drink, hates wet weather
and would rather sleep most times

My happiness is growing weary
and thinks about taking out a personal ad.
But there are lies, vague teasing,

hyperbolic flamboyance,
sad reports that counter hope,
and there's no end to it.

ABOUT THE AUTHOR

Charles Cantrell's chapbooks are *Cicatrix* and *Greatest Hits*. His awards include grants from the Wisconsin Arts Board, a scholarship from the Fine Arts Work Center, residencies from Ragdale, Ucross, the Vermont Studio Center, the Virginia Center for the Creative Arts, and three Pushcart Prize nominations. Mr. Cantrell, an Air Force veteran, received his MFA from Goddard College (now at Warren Wilson). He taught for several years at Madison Area Technical College and lives in Madison, Wisconsin with his wife and son.

www.ingramcontent.com/pod-product-compliance
Lightning Source LLC
Chambersburg PA
CBHW022205080426
42734CB00006B/556